The Kopan Cookbook

Betty Jung

The Kopan Cookbook

Vegetarian Recipes from a Tibetan Monastery

Illustrations by R.E. Peña

Chronicle Books • San Francisco

Part of the proceeds of this book will
go to the Kopan Monastery.

First published in the United States by Chronicle Books.

Originally published in Nepal in 1989.

Copyright ©1992 by Betty Jung and the Mount Everest Center

Printed in the United States of America

Library of Congress Cataloging-in-Publication Data

Jung, Betty.
    The Kopan cookbook: vegetarian recipes from a Tibetan monastery /
by Betty Jung: illustrations by Ernie Peña.
      p.   cm.
    ISBN: 0-8118-0113-6 (pbk.)
    1. Vegetarian cookery. 2. Cookery, Tibetan. 3. Kopan (Monstary:
Kathmandu, Nepal) II. Title.
TX837.J86 1992   91-44542
641.5′636 — dc20   CIP

Distributed in Canada by Raincoast Books,
112 East Third Avenue, Vancouver, B.C. V5T 1C8

10 9 8 7 6 5 4 3 2 1

Chronicle Books
275 Fifth St.
San Francisco, CA 94103

contents

I first came to Kopan, a Tibetan Buddhist monastery just outside Kathmandu, Nepal, for a fourteen-day meditation course in March 1989. However, it was not so much a spiritual search as a culinary one that had brought me to Asia. A native Californian and a graduate of the University of California, Berkeley, I was trained as a teacher and a medical technologist, but I had recently realized that my first love was cooking. So, I took a year off for an adventurous vacation to learn about the many cuisines of Asia. ❀ Before coming to Nepal I had spent three months in Thailand, where I studied Thai cuisine in Chiangmai for six weeks with a local widow. We had such a good time cooking up a storm every day that I suggested she try teaching others as well. By the end of my first week there we managed to set up cooking classes for tourists, and by the end of our second week we were in business. And so my enthusiasm grew. ❀ In Nepal, however, I decided to pursue my interest in Buddhism and meditation, so I enrolled at Kopan. It's a beautiful place. Perched on a hilltop, it has stunning, full-circle views of the Kathmandu valley below and the Himalayas beyond, clusters of homes surrounded by terraced farmland and lush green fields, and in the distance the dome-shaped Boudhanath Stupa, one of the most important Buddhist sites in Nepal. Formerly the residence of the King's astrologer, Kopan is now home for 130 Tibetan and Sherpa lamas, monks, and nuns. One of its functions is to hold Buddhist meditation courses throughout the year for Westerners. ❊ Two Buddhist lamas, Lama Thubten Yeshe (1935–1984) and Lama Thubten Zopa Rinpoche, moved here with their first Western student, Zina Rachevsky, in 1969. The lamas spent half of each year at Kopan and the other half in Lawudo, a village in Solo Khumbu near Mount Everest. Here, Lama Zopa started Mount Everest Center, fulfilling a promise made in his previous life as the Lawudo Lama to educate young Sherpa boys from the area. At first the students journeyed to Kathmandu with their lamas each winter to live and study at Kopan, returning home to Lawudo in the summer. Eventually, the center was settled permanently on Kopan Hill, and the present monastery was created. ❊ During that time, Kathmandu was a mecca for Westerners seeking, among other things, alternative spiritual and philosophical paths. They soon discovered Kopan, and Lama Zopa Rinpoche gave his first meditation course, for twelve people, in 1970. Other courses followed, and by the fifth, the attendance had swelled to 200. Western interest in Buddhism was so strong that many of the lamas' students established meditation centers in their own countries upon their return and invited the lamas to teach there. Lama Yeshe named this growing network of centers the Foundation for the Preservation of the Mahayana Tradition (FPMT), which to date comprises more than fifty centers and other activities around the world. And Kopan, where this movement began, now welcomes over 1,000 visitors every year who attend monthly courses, do meditational retreats, or simply come to stay. ❋ I was glad to be at Kopan and enjoyed the beauty of the place. My course was taught by one of the resident Tibetan lamas, Geshe Lama Könchog, and Swedish Buddhist nun Karin Valham. Our schedule was rigorous, starting at dawn, and ending around nine p.m. and consisting of at least seven sessions daily: meditation, lectures on the Buddhist path to enlightenment and group discussions. And, to my delight, the course included three meals a day! Then I discovered the food would be vegetarian. "Oh, no!" I thought. "Fourteen days of vegetarian food, I'll never make it without meat!" But to my surprise the meals were great. I was told that years ago the Kopan food was nothing to brag about, but now the cook — whom I discovered was called Kancha — seemed to understand the emphasis visiting Westerners place on food, especially during the intensive atmosphere of a meditation course. He really outdid himself in his efforts to please us: healthy wheat chapatis, tasty homemade noodles, tossed green salads, delicious soups, and homemade peanut butter and jam — a daily feast! ❋ I was so delighted that by the middle of the first week I asked Karin if there was a cookbook of Kopan recipes available. When she said no, I asked if I could help put one together. Karin, it seemed, had already asked Kancha to write a cookbook just two months earlier, but he had said that he was too busy. She agreed to ask him again, telling him that I would help. Again, he said no. I was so disappointed, but being the fighter I am, I wasn't going down without a struggle. I decided to go to the kitchen and ask him myself. So, I went with a huge smile on my face and told him I would do most of the work. How could he refuse me? ✻ I started work in the kitchen the very afternoon my course finished — I couldn't wait! I spent all day every day there for three weeks. During that time, I not only learned all about Kancha's cooking but also discovered what a delightful man he is. Unassuming and kind and completely dedicated to his job, he'd traveled a long hard road to end up at Kopan. In 1972, at the age of thirteen, he ran away from home in Eastern Nepal (he is a Tamang) to come to the big city of Kathmandu. And what a big city it was for a young boy who'd never even seen an automobile! For six months he just managed to survive by doing odd jobs — which for a thirteen-year-old untrained boy were very difficult to find. Then followed six hard months of sweat and suffering as a cycle rick-shaw driver. By now, Kancha was ready to move on — to what he didn't know. ✻ But luck was on his side. One day, one of his pas-sengers was Lama Pasang, Kopan's manager. He found Kancha a job as a kitchen hand in a local restaurant. And then, when that didn't work out, Lama Pasang invited Kancha to come and work in the kitchen at Kopan. ✻ Kancha was delighted by the serenity and beauty of Kopan, and he decided immediately that he would stay. But the following day, when he was taking food to one of Lama Zopa Rinpoche's classes, he was attacked by one of Kopan's big dogs. As well as being bitten, his pants were torn to shreds — a terrifying experience for a fourteen-year-old! He was consoled and nursed back to health by Lama Zopa and Lama Pasang, and, luckily for Kopan, Kancha stayed on. ❀ After nine years of washing dishes and chopping vegetables, Kancha was finally made head cook. A year later he married Kanchi, a woman from his own village, and now, five years later, they and their three children live in a house on Kopan Hill. ❀ What a struggle it was for me, too, getting used to Kancha's kitchen! Wood-burning earth stoves, constant smoke, massive pots and pans — including a wok that measures almost four feet across — and quantities of food for rarely less than 150 people. And everything, and I mean everything, made from scratch. Not exactly your ideal Western kitchen! How could I scale this all down for just half-a-dozen people? How would I work out the temperatures? How could I accurately assess the times? ❀ But the kitchen was also a delight to work in. Kancha, his assistant Maila, and the many monks and nuns who rotated on kitchen duty made me feel completely at home. They would always laugh at my efforts, especially when I tried to make chapatis. (I must have made 500 of them, but I still can't make one perfectly round.) ❀ The best times in the kitchen were the occasions we made momos, a Tibetan national dish.

They are everyone's favorite, and when the word got out that they were being made, there was never a shortage of volunteer momo-makers. There we'd be, eight or ten of us, rolling out the pastry wrappers and filling them. I called these fun gatherings our momo parties. ❄ So, finally the recipes are together. I want to thank Karin Valham for helping me get this project started, and Lama Lhundrup, Kopan's Lama-in-Charge, for seeing the practicality of a Kopan Cookbook and giving me the approval to do it. Thank you to all the Westerners at Kopan during the March and April courses for their interest, support and encouragement, especially: Carol Berg of New York, who took time from her three-month studies to read my first draft; Lesa Stark, a Peace Corps volunteer from Washington, who read the manuscript; and Ron Klein from Pennsylvania, who was invaluable to me during the final stages of writing. ❄ Thank you Thubten Khedrup Sherpa and Dornam from Kopan's office for letting me use Kopan's typewriter and supplies. Much love and thanks to Robina Courtin, the Australian nun, for guidance, editing, and taking the responsibility for seeing the original edition through to completion; and thank you to Hadley Brown. ❄ I couldn't have succeeded without the help, patience and loving-kindness of Maila and all the monks and nuns who worked with me, who showed me the ropes and a good time — and that you can have fun in a smoke-filled kitchen! ❄ And most of all a super big hug and thanks to Kancha for having me in his kitchen in the first place and for passing on to me all his secrets. His dedication to making people happy is an inspiration. Without him this book would still be just a passing thought. ❈ A few years ago I had the idea to write a cookbook — some day. All of these people have helped me see the seed I planted then grow into a beautiful lotus right before my eyes. And my wish is that putting together these vegetarian recipes will perhaps help me practice Dharma and be of benefit to others as well. It has been a labor of love. Kopan, thank you so much!

Betty Jung
Kopan Hill
Kathmandu
April 1989

acknowledgments

I'd also like to take a moment to thank everyone who helped make this book a reality in the West. ❀ Thanks to all my friends and family for their support. Special thanks to Dale Binkley for his encouragement, Debbie Matsumoto for her advice, and Charlotte Stone at Chronicle for her patience and understanding — sorry I missed so many deadlines! I'm especially indebted to Meesha Halm, Chronicle's Food Consultant, for assisting me in retesting and revising the recipes for the Western audience and palate. To Ernie Peña, who's also been at Kopan and knows how special a place it is, for his beautiful Tibetan Buddhist illustrations. And to Nion McEvoy, Chronicle's Editor-in-Chief, whose excitement about the book refueled me and kept me going. ❀ You've all touched my heart with your love and kindness. Thanks again from the bottom of my heart for helping me see one of my dreams come true.

— November 1991
Reedley, CA

This book is dedicated to my mom, my favorite cook,
who has always been an inspiration to me in the kitchen.

I've taken a selection of Kancha's dishes — which he has developed over the years with a style and a flair all his own — and divided them into the following sections: appetizers, soups, rice dishes, noodle dishes, breads, condiments, and teas. I've done my best to scale them down for four-to-six people — if they happen to feed more, just think what great leftovers you'll have! Cooking times are approximate, so please use common sense. ✹ Kancha usually uses parboiled vegetables, so remember to make adjustments to cooking times if you choose raw vegetables: add more water to soups, for example, or stir-fry a little longer. If you do parboil the vegetables, don't forget to rinse them with cool water to prevent them from over-cooking. As to which vegetables to use, do as Kancha does: use whatever's in season. ✹ With spices and seasonings, however, I have tried to be more precise. For instance, Kancha uses fresh ginger root only — powdered ginger is made from the leaves of the ginger plant and gives an entirely different flavor. Please remember that whole spices are always stronger and more flavorful than the packaged varieties. I'm sure the more exotic spices can be purchased in Asian or Indian grocery stores (see the glossary of spices on page 110). Also, Kancha uses a Chinese-style soy sauce, which is stronger than, say Japanese tamari, so adjust amounts if necessary. ✹ I've not seen white or yellow onions used in Asia. At Kopan, Kancha always uses red onions, which are mild and sweet, so if you use the former kinds, use less because they are stronger. ✳ The yeast we use is the fresh, moist, cubed variety found in the refrigerated or deli section at your local grocer. ✳ The cheese used at Kopan was yak cheese. Since it's not available in the West, comparable substitutes are Swiss, Jack or Mozzerella cheese. ✳ Perhaps I should clarify a few terms. Tofu is also known as bean curd, a fresh soy bean product available in all shapes, sizes, and firmnesses, and a high source of protein. Green onions are also known as spring onions or scallions. Skillet, it seems, is American for frying pan. ✳ And throughout, I have used measuring cups and spoons, but if you are at a loss, a tablespoon is approximately the same as an English dessert spoon. ✳ Enjoy!

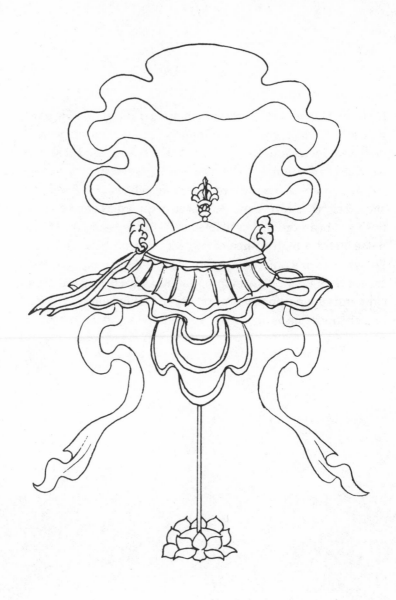

*appetizers

momo wrappers _____

Makes approximately 18

2 ½ c. flour (white or half white and half wheat)
¼ tsp. baking powder
Pinch of salt
¾ c. water

* *method*

*Pour flour in a mound on a counter or in a mixing
bowl. Make a hole in the center.* ☾ *Sprinkle baking
powder and salt on top.* ☾ *Pour half the water into
the hole. With your hand mix the water with the
flour. Work in a circular motion until it is well mixed.
Add the second half of water and repeat the process
until everything is thoroughly mixed and well incorporated.* ☾ *Knead well for at least 5 minutes. Cover
and set aside for 30 minutes.* ☾ *On a well-floured
surface knead the dough for a few minutes. With both
hands, roll dough into a long sausage shape about 1
inch in diameter. Cut into pieces 1 inch wide, or about
the width of one finger. The pieces should look like and*

be the size of sea scallops. ☾ Dust with flour and flatten each piece into rounds with the palm of your hand. ☾ Place your right palm on the center of a rolling pin. With your left hand holding a piece of dough on the counter, slowly roll over the dough just rolling in ⅓ of the way. As you roll out, rotate the dough and roll in again ⅓. Repeat this process until the wrapper is round and approximately 3-3½ inches in diameter with the thickness of a coin. The center of the wrapper should be a little thicker than the edges; this is to prevent the fillings from leaking out during the cooking process. ☾ Fill with wonderful delights! Steam, pan-fry or deep-fry.

*An alternative: Try using won ton wrappers or pot sticker wrappers. Makes approximately 50. ☾ Place 1 tsp. momo filling on one half of the wrapper. Fold in half into a triangle or half-moon. Seal with a dab of egg. ☾ Pan-fry or deep fry until golden brown. Delicious!

This is the basic pastry used for most momos. Momos are Tibetan dumplings that are filled with wonderful delights, then steamed. They make a delicious appetizer. A great starter to any meal!

p o t a t o   m o m o s _____

✳ i n g r e d i e n t s

Makes approximately 18

¼ c. butter
½ Tbsp. fresh ginger root, minced
½ Tbsp. fresh garlic, minced
¼ c. red onion, diced
½ tsp. Kopan masala (see page 92)
½ tsp. chili powder
¼ tsp. salt
¼ tsp. ground black pepper
1 Tbsp. soy sauce
2 c. mashed potato
½ c. fresh spinach, parboiled and chopped (optional)
¼ c. Chinese parsley/cilantro, finely chopped
¼ c. green onion, finely chopped
momo wrappers (see page 16)
1 large egg
momo sauce (see page 26)

*For potato cheese momos, substitute spinach with
1½ c. mild white cheeese (Jack or Mozzerella), grated,
and omit Masala. If the cheese you are using tends to
be a bit on the salty side, you may want to reduce or
omit the salt in this recipe.*

Melt butter in a small skillet over medium heat. ✧ *Add ginger, garlic, and red onion and stir-fry for 1 minute over medium to medium-high heat.* ✧ *Add masala, chili powder, salt, black pepper, and soy sauce and stir-fry for another half minute.* ✧ *Remove from heat and in a bowl combine this mixture with the mashed potatoes.* ✧ *When the potato mixture has cooled, add spinach, if desired (or cheese* for potato cheese momos), Chinese parsley and green onion. Mix well. Salt to taste.* ✧ *Put 1 Tbsp. of potato mixture in the center of a momo wrapper, pull the sides up around the filling and pinch closed (see illustration below), or fold in half. Seal with a dab of egg.* ✧ *Grease steaming rack with oil. Place momos 1-2 inches apart. Steam for 15-20 minutes. Serve hot with momo sauce.*

※ *method*

For potato momos or potato cheese momos

Cooking variations: Pan-fry like pot stickers. ○ *Add 1-2 Tbsp. vegetable oil to a skillet. Pan-fry momos on medium heat until each side is golden brown.* ○ *Add either ¼ c. water to skillet if using won ton wrappers or ½ c. if using the thicker pot sticker wrapper, cover and allow to steam until water evaporates.* ○ *Serve hot. Or deep-fry until golden brown.*

The monastery's favorite!

spinach cheese momos _____

❋ *ingredients*

Makes approximately 18

2 c. fresh spinach, parboiled, chopped and squeezed
2 c. mild white cheese (Jack or Mozzarella), grated
¼ c. melted butter
momo wrappers (see page 16)
1 large egg
momo sauce (see page 26)

※ *m e t h o d*

Boil spinach and allow to cool. ☾ *In a medium bowl, combine the spinach, cheese, and melted butter. Mix well.* ☾ *Put 1 Tbsp. of mixture in the center of a momo wrapper, pull the sides up around the filling and pinch closed or fold in half. Seal with a dab of egg.* ☾ *Grease steaming rack with oil. Place momos 1-2 inches apart.* ☾ *Steam for 15-20 minutes. Serve hot with momo sauce.*

Cooking variations: *Pan-fry like pot stickers.* ☾ *Add 1-2 Tbsp. Vegetable oil to a skillet. Pan-fry momos on medium heat until each side is golden brown.* ☾ *Add either ¼ c. water to skillet using won ton wrappers or ½ c. if using the thicker pot sticker wrapper, cover and allow to steam until water evaporates.* ☾ *Serve hot. Or deep-fry until golden brown.*

vegetable momos _____

Makes approximately 18

2 Tbsp. vegetable oil
½ Tbsp. fresh ginger root, minced
½ Tbsp. fresh garlic, minced
½ c. red onion, diced
1 tsp. Kopan masala (see page 92)
½ tsp. chili powder
¼ tsp. ground black pepper
¼ tsp. salt
1 Tbsp. soy sauce
2 c. mixed vegetables, parboiled and finely chopped (for example, carrot,
    spinach, green pepper, cabbage, cauliflower)
1 c. tofu, squeezed and crumbled
momo wrappers (see page 16)
1 large egg
momo sauce (see page 26)

✴ *m e t h o d*

Melt oil in wok or skillet over medium heat. ✦ *Add
ginger, garlic, and red onion. Stir-fry for 1 minute*

over medium to medium-high heat. ✧ Add masala, chili powder, black pepper, salt, and soy sauce. Stir-fry for another half minute. ✧ Add vegetables. Stir-fry a few minutes more until mixed well. ✧ Remove from heat and place in a bowl. ✧ Add tofu. Toss well. ✧ Allow mixture to cool and drain off excess liquid. ✧ Put 1 Tbsp. of vegetable mixture in the center of a momo wrapper, pull the sides up around the filling and pinch closed, or fold in half. Seal with a dab of egg. ✧ Grease steaming rack with oil. Place momos 1-2 inches apart. ✧ Steam for 15-20 minutes. Serve hot with momo sauce.

Cooking variations: *Pan-fry like pot stickers. ✧ Add 1-2 Tbsp. vegetable oil to a skillet. Pan-fry momos on medium heat until each side is golden brown. ✧ Add either ¼ c. water to skillet if using won ton wrappers or ½ c. if using the thicker pot sticker wrapper, cover and allow to steam until water evaporates. ✧ Serve hot. Or deep-fry until golden brown.*

Another delectable variation.

Makes 1½ cups

2 Tbsp. vegetable oil
1 tsp. fresh ginger root, minced
1 tsp. fresh garlic, minced
½ c. red onion, diced
½ tsp. Kopan masala (see page 92)
⅛ tsp. turmeric
½ tsp. chili powder
1 c. fresh tomatoes, diced
1 c. water
½ tsp. white vinegar
1 tsp. soy sauce
¼ tsp. salt
¼ tsp. ground black pepper
green onions, finely chopped
2 sprigs of Chinese parsley/cilantro, finely chopped

Heat oil in a small saucepan over medium heat. ○
Add ginger, garlic, and red onion. Stir-fry over
medium to medium-high heat for ½-1 minute. ○
Add masala, turmeric and chili powder. Continue to
stir-fry half minute more. ○ *Add tomatoes and stir*
fry 2-3 minutes. ○ *Add water. Bring to boil.*
Simmer for 5 minutes. ○ *Add vinegar, soy sauce,*
salt, and pepper to taste. Mix well. ○ *Garnish with*
green onions and Chinese parsley. Serve hot.

Kancha's momo sauce, a necessity when eating
momos.

Makes 1½ cups

spring roll wrappers _____

Makes 20

⅓ c. white flour
⅓ c. cornstarch
pinch of salt
1 large egg
1 c. water

Mix flour, cornstarch, and salt in a small bowl. ☾
*Add egg and water. Mix well with a wire whisk until
batter is super smooth and without lumps (should be
the consistency of milk). Put aside 1-2 Tbsp. of batter
for use as a sealant when making the spring
rolls.* ☾ *Heat a 12-inch skillet over medium heat. For
best results, use a teflon surface. Pour a few drops of
vegetable oil into the skillet and spread with a pastry
brush.* ☾ *The skillet should be lightly greased.*
☾ *Add batter to the skillet and swirl quickly over the*

entire surface, forming a thin even layer. Quickly pour excess back into bowl. ☾ Cook over low-medium heat. Wrapper is done when the edges begin to pull away from the sides of the skillet. ☾ Turn pan upside down over counter or cutting board and let wrapper fall. When wrapper is cool to touch, cut into quarters. ☾ Set aside.

Kancha is the only person I know who makes his own spring roll wrappers!

spring rolls

Makes 20

2 Tbsp. vegetable oil
½ Tbsp. fresh ginger, minced
½ Tbsp. fresh garlic, minced
½ c. red onion, diced
1 c. fresh bean sprouts
*2 c. mixed vegetables, parboiled, finely chopped or shredded (broccoli,
    cabbage, carrots, cauliflower, mushrooms, spinach, squash)*
1 Tbsp. soy sauce
¼ tsp. salt
¼ tsp. ground black pepper
1 c. tofu, squeezed and crumbled
¼ c. Chinese parsley/cilantro, finely chopped (optional)
20 spring roll wrappers
oil for deep frying

❉ *method*

Heat oil in a wok over medium heat. ✧ *Add ginger,
garlic and red onion. Stir-fry for 1 minute over*

medium to medium-high heat. ✧ Add bean sprouts.
Stir-fry for 1 minute then add mixed vegetables. Mix
well and continue to stir-fry 1-2 more minutes. ✧
Add soy sauce, salt, and pepper to taste. ✧ Remove
from heat and place in a bowl. ✧ Add tofu and Chinese parsley, if desired. Toss well. ✧ Allow mixture
to cool and drain off excess liquid. ✧ Place 1 Tbsp.
of filling at the large end of the triangular spring roll
wrapper. ✧ Bring bottom edge over filling and roll
over once. Fold ends in and continue to roll half way.
Make sure roll is tight, but be careful not to tear the
wrapper. ✧ Apply a little left-over wrapper batter or
egg to the edges of the open end. Continue to roll shut.
✧ Heat oil in wok over medium to medium high
heat. Put a wooden utensil into the oil to test the temperature: If bubbles form, oil is ready. Slide spring
rolls in one by one. ✧ Deep fry, several at a time,
until golden brown. This should take about 1-2 minutes. Lower heat if necessary. ✧ Remove and drain
on paper towels. Serve hot.

A delightful bite-size deep-fried roll with a vegetable
filling.

omelette sandwich _____

Makes 4 small omelettes

4 eggs
⅛ c. red onion, diced
1 Tbsp. green onion, finely chopped
1 Tbsp. Chinese parsley/cilantro, finely chopped
1-2 Tbsp. fresh tomato, diced
Salt and pepper to taste
4 Kopan chapatis (see page 74)

Beat eggs in small bowl. ○ *Add all ingredients (except chapatis). Mix well.* ○ *Warm a small skillet over medium heat. Slightly grease pan.* ○ *Add egg mixture and swirl over entire surface of skillet, forming a thin layer of egg. Pour excess back into bowl.* ○ *Cook over medium heat. When the edges begin to pull away from the side of the skillet, turn omelette over. Continue to cook just a few more seconds. Remove from heat.* ○ *Repeat process with the rest of egg mixture.* ○ *Serve hot in a warm folded chapati.*

A tasty, filling breakfast.

cheese stick pakoras

Makes 16

½ lb. hard white mild cheese (Swiss)
⅔ c. white flour
¼ tsp. baking powder
½ tsp. salt
¼ tsp. ground black pepper
1 egg
½ c. water
Pinch of Indian Tomato Red Powder (see page 111) (optional)
oil for deep frying

Cut cheese into bite-size sticks, approximately 3 inches long by half inch wide. ❨ Mix all dry ingredients in a small bowl. Add egg and water. Mix well with a wire whisk. ❨ Dip cheese stick in batter until well coated. ❨ Heat oil in a wok over medium heat. Put a wooden utensil into the oil to test the temperature: when bubbles form, oil is ready. Add coated cheese sticks one by one. ❨ Lower heat and cook for 2-3 minutes or until the cheese begins to bubble and ooze through the coating. ❨ Remove and drain on paper towels. Serve hot.

Wonderful deep-fried cheese delights.

vegetable pakoras _____

Makes 18

1 c. flour
¼ tsp. baking powder
2 eggs
½ c. water
1 Tbsp. fresh ginger root, minced
1 Tbsp. fresh garlic, minced
¼ c. red onion, sliced thin in semi-circles
¼ c. Chinese parsley/cilantro, finely chopped
1 tsp. Kopan masala (see page 92)
¼ tsp. chili powder
½ tsp. salt
¼ tsp. ground black pepper
2 tsp. soy sauce
Pinch of Indian Tomato Red Powder (see page 111) (optional)
2 c. fresh cauliflower/fresh broccoli — flowerets only, sliced thin,
    or 2 c. mixed vegetables, shredded or julienne (bell pepper, cabbage,
    carrots, green beans, squash)
oil for deep frying

In a bowl, mix flour, baking powder, egg, and water until smooth by using a wire whisk. ✧ *Add spices, seasonings, red powder, and red onion. Mix well.* ✧ *Add vegetables to batter and coat well.* ✧ *Heat oil in wok. Put a wooden utensil into the oil to test the temperature: when bubbles form, oil is ready.* ✧ *Add heaping tablespoons of coated floweret clusters or vegetable clusters one by one.* ✧ *Deep-fry on medium to medium-high heat until golden brown.* ✧ *Remove and drain on paper towels.* ✧ *Serve hot.*

A spicy deep-fried vegetable cluster similar to Japanese tempura.

✻ *s o u p s*

p o t a t o   s o u p

Serves 4

¼ c. butter
1 Tbsp. fresh ginger root, minced
1 Tbsp. fresh garlic, minced
1 c. red onion, diced
½ tsp. turmeric
½ tsp. chili powder
½ tsp. Kopan masala (see page 92)
3 c. mashed potato
4 c. water
1 c. tofu, diced
1 c. fresh spinach, chopped
½ Tbsp. white vinegar
1 Tbsp. soy sauce
2 tsp. salt
½ tsp. ground black pepper
⅛ c. green onion, chopped
⅛ c. Chinese parsley/cilantro, chopped

Melt butter in a large saucepan over medium heat.
☾ *Add ginger, garlic, and red onion. Stir-fry over
medium to medium-high heat for ½-1 minute.* ☾
*Add turmeric, chili powder, and masala. Stir-fry ½
minute more.* ☾ *Add mashed potatoes and mix
again. Continue to stir and cook 3 more minutes.*
☾ *Add water, 1 cup at a time, stirring constantly
with a wire whisk to prevent lumps from forming.
Stir until mixture is smooth.* ☾ *Add tofu and spinach. Mix well and bring to a boil.* ☾ *Add vinegar,
soy sauce, salt, and pepper to taste.* ☾ *Allow to
simmer for 5 more minutes. If soup is too thick, add
water.* ☾ *Garnish with green onions and Chinese
parsley. A must! Mix well.* ☾ *Remove from heat and
serve hot.*

Possibly the best potato soup ever! A Kopan favorite.

p u m p k i n   s o u p _____

☀ *i n g r e d i e n t s*

Serves 4

¼ c. butter
1 Tbsp. fresh ginger root, minced
½ c. red onion, diced
¼ c. white flour
3 c. pumpkin, cooked and mashed
4-5 c. water
½ tsp. ground cinnamon
¼ tsp. ground nutmeg
1 Tbsp. sugar
½ Tbsp. soy sauce
1 tsp. salt
¼ tsp. ground black pepper
¼ tsp. chili powder
¼ c. green onion, chopped

Peel and cube pumpkin. Boil or bake until soft, then mash. ✧ *Melt butter in a large saucepan over medium heat.* ✧ *Add ginger and red onion. Stir-fry over medium to medium-high heat for 1 minute.* ✧ *Lower heat. Add flour and continue to stir until flour mixture is slightly golden in color, 3-5 minutes.* ✧ *Add mashed pumpkin and mix well.* ✧ *Add water 1 cup at a time, stirring constantly with a wire whisk to prevent lumps from forming. Stir until mixture is smooth.* ✧ *Bring to boil and add spices and seasonings to taste.* ✧ *Allow to boil for 2-3 minutes more. Add green onion and mix well. If soup is too thick, add more water.* ✧ *Remove from heat and serve hot.*

Pumpkins in Asia? A nice surprise!

corn soup

✸ *ingredients*

Serves 4

2 Tbsp. butter
1 tsp. fresh ginger root, minced
1 tsp. fresh garlic, minced
¼ c. red onion, diced
½ tsp. turmeric
½ tsp. chili powder
2 c. creamed corn (canned)
½ c. tofu, diced
½ c. milk
½ c. water
½ Tbsp. soy sauce
½ tsp. salt
½ tsp. ground black pepper
green onion, chopped (optional)

Melt butter in a large saucepan over medium heat.
○ *Add ginger, garlic, and red onion. Stir-fry over
medium to medium-high heat for 1 minute.* ○ *Add
turmeric and chili powder. Mix well.* ○ *Add corn
and tofu. Mix well and continue to cook for 1 minute*
○ *Add milk and water. Continue to stir until soup
comes to the boil. Lower heat and allow to simmer for
5 minutes.* ○ *Season with soy sauce, salt, and pepper to taste.* ○ *Remove from heat and serve hot.*
○ *Garnished with green onion, if desired.*

A fresh idea for creamed corn.

*vegetable soup*_____

Serves 4

2 Tbsp. butter
1 Tbsp. fresh ginger root, minced
1 Tbsp. fresh garlic, minced
½ c. red onion, diced
¼ c. white flour
4 c. water
2 c. mixed vegetables, parboiled and chopped
½ c. fresh tomatoes, diced
1 c. tofu, diced
¼ c. green onion, chopped
1 Tbsp. soy sauce
1 tsp. salt
¼ tsp. ground black pepper

Melt butter in large saucepan over medium heat. ☾ Add ginger, garlic, and red onion. Stir-fry over medium to medium-high heat for 1 minute. ☾ Add flour and continue to stir until flour mixture is slightly golden in color, 3-5 minutes. ☾ Add water 1 cup at a time, stirring constantly with a wire whisk to prevent lumps from forming. Stir until mixture is smooth. ☾ Add vegetables, tomatoes, tofu and green onions. Bring to the boil. Add soy sauce, salt, and pepper to taste. ☾ Allow to boil for 2-3 minutes. If soup is too thick, add water. ☾ Remove from heat and serve hot.

A gardener's delight!

spinach egg drop soup _____

✳ *ingredients*

Serves 4

2 Tbsp. butter
1 Tbsp. fresh ginger root, minced
1 Tbsp. fresh garlic, minced
½ c. red onion, diced
¼ c. white flour
4 c. water
1-1½ c. fresh spinach, chopped
½ cup fresh tomatoes, chopped
½ c. tofu, diced
1 Tbsp. soy sauce
½ tsp. chili powder
1 tsp. salt
¼ tsp. ground black pepper
1 egg

*Melt butter in a large saucepan over medium heat.
✧ Add ginger, garlic, and red onion. Stir-fry over
medium to medium-high heat for 1 minute. ✧ Add
flour and continue to stir until flour mixture is slightly
golden in color, approximately 3-5 minutes. ✧ Add
water 1 cup at a time, stirring constantly with a wire
whisk to prevent lumps from forming. Stir until
mixture is smooth. ✧ Add spinach, tomatoes, and
tofu. Mix well and bring to the boil. ✧ Add soy
sauce, chili powder, salt, and pepper to taste. ✧
Allow to boil for 1-2 more minutes. If soup is too thick,
add water. ✧ In a small bowl, lightly beat egg. Just
before serving, gradually add egg to soup, stirring
constantly. ✧ Remove from heat and serve hot.*

Popeye would have loved this!

*rice dishes

dal

☀ *ingredients*

Serves 4

1 c. dry lentils, black or yellow
⅛ c. vegetable oil
½ c. red onion, diced
1 Tbsp. fresh ginger root, minced
1 Tbsp. fresh garlic, minced
1 tsp. turmeric
1 tsp. chili powder
1 tsp. Kopan masala (see page 92)
4 c. water
¼ c. green onion, chopped
2 Tbsp. Chinese parsley/cilantro, chopped
1 tsp. salt

Rinse lentils 2-3 times with cool water. Cover with water and set aside for 1 hour. ☾ *Heat oil in a large saucepan over a medium heat.* ☾ *Add red onion, ginger, garlic, turmeric, chili powder and masala. Stir-fry over medium to medium-high heat for 1 minute.* ☾ *Drain and add lentils and continue to stir-fry for 2-3 minutes.* ☾ *Add water and bring to the boil. Allow to simmer over low to medium-low heat for 30 minutes, or until lentils are soft. Add more water if dal becomes too thick.* ☾ *Salt to taste.* ☾ *Just before serving, add green onion and Chinese parsley. Mix well.* ☾ *Serve hot.*

A lentil-based staple of Indian and Nepali cuisines.

vegetable curry _____

Serves 4

2 Tbsp. vegetable oil
½ tsp. cumin seeds, crushed
½ tsp. coriander seeds, crushed
1 Tbsp. fresh ginger root, minced
1 Tbsp. fresh garlic, minced
½ c. red onion, diced
1 tsp. turmeric
1 tsp. Kopan masala (see page 92)
1 tsp. hot curry powder
½ tsp. chili powder
2 bay leaves
2 c. mixed vegetables, parboiled, chopped or bite-size (broccoli, carrot,
    cauliflower, squash, string beans)
1 c. potato, parboiled and cubed
1 c. fresh tomatoes, chopped
1 c. water
1 tsp. white vinegar
1 Tbsp. soy sauce
1 tsp. salt
¼ tsp. ground black pepper

Heat oil in large saucepan over medium heat. ✧ *Add cumin, coriander, ginger, garlic, and red onion. Stir-fry for 1 minute over medium to medium-high heat.* ✧ *Add turmeric, masala, curry powder, chili powder, and bay leaves. Mix well.* ✧ *Add vegetables, potatoes, tomatoes, and tofu. Mix well and stir-fry for 2 more minutes.* ✧ *Add water and bring to boil. Simmer for 3-5 minutes.* ✧ *Season with vinegar, soy sauce, salt, and pepper to taste.* ✧ *Remove from heat and serve hot.*

Traditionally served with rice and dal. Be sure to use the best curry available.

red pulau: indian fried rice

✳ ingredients

Serves 6

3 black cardamom pods
6 pale green cardamom pods
½ cinnamon stick
6 cloves
¼ c. butter
½ c. red onion, diced
1 c. fresh or frozen peas
1 c. raisins, presoaked in water
1 c. cashew nuts
2 bay leaves
6 c. long-grain white rice, steamed*
2 c. mixed vegetables, parboiled and chopped or shredded (for example, cabbage, cauliflower, carrot, spinach, broccoli)
½ c. fresh tomatoes, diced
Dash of Indian Tomato Red Powder, (optional) (see page 111)
1 tsp. salt
1½ Tbsp. sugar
1 c. coconut flakes

Peel and discard the outer skin of cardamom pods. With a mortar and pestle, rolling pin, or grinder, crush the cardamom seeds, cinnamon stick, and cloves. Put the coarsely ground spices in 1 Tbsp. warm water. Allow to soak for 15 minutes. ○ *Heat butter in wok over medium heat.* ○ *Add red onion and stir-fry over medium-high heat for 1 minute.* ○ *Add peas, raisins, cashews, and bay leaves and stir-fry for 1 more minute.* ☾ *Add cooked rice. Mix well.* ☾ *Add spiced water mixture and continue to stir-fry. When the rice has absorbed all the water, add vegetables and tomatoes. Mix well.* ○ *Add Tomato Red Powder, salt and sugar, and continue to stir-fry until thoroughly mixed.* ○ *Remove from heat.* ○ *Add coconut flakes. Toss lightly. Serve hot.*

*Day-old rice is much easier to stir-fry than freshly cooked rice because it is less sticky.

This rice dish is not only pleasing and beautiful to the eye, but also one of the best fried rice dishes I have ever tasted!

cashew rice

✵ *ingredients*

Serves 6

6 c. long-grain white rice, steamed
⅓ c. vegetable oil
2 c. red onion, thinly sliced in semi-circles
1 c. fresh or frozen peas
½ c. carrot, shredded
1½ c. cashew nuts
1 c. raisins, presoaked in water
salt to taste

✹ *m e t h o d*

Heat ⅓ cup oil in a wok over medium to medium-high heat. ☾ Add 1 cup of red onion and deep-fry until crispy. Remove onion. Set aside. Repeat with second cup. ☾ Pour off excess oil, leaving 2 Tbsp. in wok. Add peas, carrots, raisins, and cashew nuts. Stir-fry 1-2 minutes. Remove from heat. ☾ Add stir-fried mixture and crispy deep-fried onions to freshly steamed rice. Toss. ☾ Salt to taste. Serve hot.

My second favorite rice dish.

kopan fried rice _____

Serves 6

oil for deep frying
½ c. tofu*
2 Tbsp. vegetable oil
1 Tbsp. fresh ginger root, minced
1 Tbsp. fresh garlic, minced
½ c. red onion, diced
¾ c. fresh or frozen peas
6 c. long-grain white rice, steamed**
2 c. mixed vegetables, parboiled, chopped or shredded (broccoli, cabbage,
    carrot, cauliflower, spinach, squash)
⅓ c. fresh tomatoes, diced
½ c. red kidney beans (fresh cooked or canned)
½ c. green onions, chopped
¼ c. Chinese parsley/cilantro, chopped
1 tsp. white vinegar
2 Tbsp. soy sauce
1 tsp. salt
¼ tsp. ground black pepper

60   kopan fried rice

Cut tofu into julienne pieces. ✧ *Heat oil (for deep frying) in a wok. Put a wooden utensil into oil to test the temperature: when bubbles form, oil is ready.* ✧ *Add tofu and fry for a few minutes on medium to medium-high heat until golden brown.* ✧ *Remove and drain on paper towels.* ✧ *Heat other oil in a wok over medium heat.* ✧ *Add ginger, garlic, and red onion. Stir-fry for 1 minute over medium to medium-high heat.* ✧ *Add peas and rice. Stir-fry for 1 more minute.* ✧ *Add vegetables, tomatoes, and beans, stir-frying until mixed well.* ✧ *Add fried tofu, green onion, and Chinese parsley during the last moments of stir-frying.* ✧ *Add vinegar, soy sauce, salt, and pepper to taste.* ✧ *Remove from heat and serve hot.*

*Best to use firm tofu made for stir-frying as it contains less water.

**Day-old rice is much easier to stir-fry than fresh rice because it is less sticky.

Better than any fried rice you've had in a restaurant.

� noodle dishes

egg noodles

Makes approximately 1 lb.

3 c. flour (white or ½ white and ½ wheat)
4 eggs
pinch of salt

Pour flour into a mound on a counter or cutting board. Make a hole in the center. ☾ *Break eggs into the hole. Mix eggs well with a fork or with your hand. Add salt.* ☾ *Working in a circular motion, gradually mix flour and eggs until the mixture is moist and smooth.* ☾ *Press dough tightly together. Knead lightly to form a smooth ball. Cover and set aside for 30 minutes.* ☾ *Flatten the dough with a rolling pin. Fold the dough in half and flatten again. Repeat several times.* ☾ *When the dough is firm and not falling apart, put it through the noodle machine. Adjust the machine to desired size: for chow mein, long, thin, and round like spaghetti; for tukpa, flat, thick, short, and rectangular like fettucini.* ☾ *Separate the noodles and spread on paper towels (Tibetans hang them over a wooden pole).*

All the noodles eaten at Kopan are made fresh every day. Now is your chance to use that noodle machine!

t u k p a :   t i b e t a n   n o o d l e   s o u p _____

✳ *i n g r e d i e n t s*

Serves 4

¼ c. butter

1½ Tbsp. fresh ginger root, minced

1½ Tbsp. fresh garlic, minced

1 c. red onion, diced

1 tsp. turmeric

1 tsp. curry powder

1 tsp. chili powder

1 tsp. Kopan masala (see page 92)

1 c. potato, parboiled and cubed

1 c. fresh tomatoes, chopped

4-5 c. water

¼ lb. fresh flat egg noodles

   or 1 c. short medium flat dry egg noodles

1½ c. fresh spinach, chopped

1-2 Tbsp. soy sauce

1 tsp. salt

¼ tsp. ground black pepper

Melt butter in a saucepan over medium heat. ✧ *Add ginger, garlic, and red onion. Stir-fry over medium to medium-high heat for 1 minute.* ✧ *Add turmeric, curry powder, chili powder, and masala. Mix well and stir fry for ½ a minute.* ✧ *Add potatoes and tomatoes. Stir-fry 1 more minute.* ✧ *Add water and bring to a boil.* ✧ *Add egg noodles and boil for 5 minutes. Stir occasionally.* ✧ *Add spinach and boil for another 1-2 minutes. If soup is too thick, add more water.* ✧ *Season with soy sauce. Salt and pepper to taste.* ✧ *Remove from heat and serve hot.*

A traditional Tibetan dish, often served as the evening meal.

kopan chow mein _____

✤ *ingredients*

Serves 4

oil for deep frying
½ c. tofu*
1 lb. fresh egg noodles
¼ c. vegetable oil
½ Tbsp. fresh ginger root, minced
½ Tbsp. fresh garlic, minced
½ c. red onion, diced
½ c. fresh or frozen peas
1 c. fresh spinach, chopped
1 c. fresh bean sprouts
3 c. mixed vegetables, parboiled and chopped
½ tsp. chili powder (optional)
1-2 Tbsp. ketchup (optional)
1-2 Tbsp. soy sauce
½ tsp. salt
¼ tsp. ground black pepper

Cut tofu into julienne pieces. ○ *Heat oil (for deep frying) in a wok. Put a wooden utensil into oil to test the temperature: when bubbles form, oil is ready.* ○ *Add tofu and fry for a few minutes on medium to medium-high heat until golden brown.* ○ *Remove and drain on paper towels.* ○ *In a large saucepan, bring water to a boil. Add noodles. When noodles float to the top, cook 1-2 minutes more. (Noodles will be cooked again, so don't overcook now.)* ○ *Drain and rinse in cool water. Add 1 teaspoon of oil and toss so they won't stick together.* ○ *Heat 2-3 tablespoons oil in a wok or skillet over medium heat.* ○ *Add 1-2 handfuls of noodles. Pan-fry (do not stir) over medium to medium-high heat. Cook until slightly crispy and golden brown, then flip over. Cook this side until crispy and golden brown.* ○ *Remove and drain on a paper towel.* ○ *Repeat the process with remaining noodles. Set aside 15-20 minutes for this step.* ○ *Heat another 1-2 tablespoons of oil in a wok over medium heat.* ○ *Add ginger, garlic, and red onion. Stir-fry for 1 minute over medium to medium-high heat.* ○ *Add bean sprouts. Mix well and stir-fry for*

*another minute. ◯ Add peas and spinach. Continue
to stir-fry ½ a minute. Then add the mixed vegetables
and fried tofu. Stir-fry 1-2 minutes more. ◯ Add
pan-fried noodles and mix well. ◯ Add seasonings
to taste and continue to stir-fry for 1 minute. ◯
Remove from heat and serve hot.*

**It's best to use firm tofu made for stir-frying as it
contains less water.*

*Chow mein is a pan-fried noodle dish eaten through-
out Asia.*

*breads

kopan chapatis _____

Makes 18

5 c. flour (white or ½ white and ½ wheat)
1 tsp. baking powder
1 tsp. fresh yeast
1½ c. warm water

❋ *method*

Pour flour in a mound on a counter or in a mixing bowl. Make a hole in the center. ☾ Sprinkle baking powder on top and crumble yeast into the hole. ☾ Pour half the amount of warm water into the hole. With your hand mix the yeast and the water and gradually work in flour from the top of the mound. Work in a circular motion until water, yeast, and dry ingredients are well mixed. Add second half of water and repeat the process until everything is thoroughly mixed. ☾ Knead well for at least 5 minutes. The dough should be well incorporated, not sticky. Cover and set aside in a warm place for 1 hour. ☾ On a well-floured surface knead the dough for a few minutes. With both hands roll the dough into a long sausage shape about 1½ inches in diameter. Cut into pieces 1 inch wide, or about the width of 2 fingers. ℭ Dust with flour and flatten each piece into a round shape with the palm of your hand. ℭ With rolling pin, roll out to approximately 6 inches in diameter (or to desired size and thickness). ℭ Warm a cast-iron griddle or skillet over medium heat. ℭ Remove excess flour from chapati by tossing it back and forth in your hands. Place one at a time on the hot griddle. ℭ When the chapati begins to form bubbles (similar to pancakes), turn it over and cook the other side. (If you have a gas stove, continue to cook over a low open flame, rotating and flipping over frequently until large bubbles form.) Continue to turn until done, 4-5 minutes. Serve hot. ℭ Excellent topped with butter, peanut butter, or jam.

A heavier chapati similar in size and weight to Middle Eastern pocket bread.

fried chapatis

✹ *ingredients*

Makes 18

follow recipe for kopan chapatis, adding:
½ c. sugar
½ tsp. salt
have oil on hand for deep frying

Follow recipe for Kopan Chapatis until you have several 6-inch pieces (or your desired size and thickness). ○ *Heat oil in a wok over medium-high heat. Put a wooden utensil into the oil to test the temperature: when bubbles form, the oil is ready.* ○ *Remove excess flour from the chapati by tossing it back and forth in your hands. Holding a chapati with both hands, carefully slide it in from the side of the wok to prevent oil from splattering.* ○ *As soon as the chapati begins to float, spoon hot oil over the top. Turn after 30 seconds. Continue to turn every 30 seconds, until golden brown, 2-2½ minutes.* ○ *Remove and drain on paper towels.* ○ *Best when served hot.*

A deep-fried sweet chapati to enjoy with tea.

indian chapatis _____

Makes 18

5 c. flour (white or ½ white and ½ wheat)
1½ c. water

Pour flour in a mound on a counter or in a mixing bowl. Make a hole in the center. ✧ *Pour half the amount of water into the hole. With your hand mix the flour and water, working from the top of the mound. Work in a circular motion. Add the second half of water and repeat the process until flour and water are thoroughly mixed.* ✧ *Knead for a least 5 minutes. The dough should be well incorporated, not sticky. Cover and set aside 30 minutes.* ✧ *On a well-floured surface, knead the dough a few minutes. With both hands roll dough into a long sausage shape 1½ inches in diameter. Cut into pieces 1 inch wide, or about the width of 2 fingers.* ✧ *Dust with flour and flatten into a round shape with the palm of your* hand. ✧ Roll out as thin as possible to approximately 8 inches in diameter. Remove excess flour by tossing chapati back and forth in your hands, at the same time stretching the dough, making it even thinner — try to make it as thin as paper. ✧ Heat a cast-iron griddle or skillet. Place one chapati at a time on hot griddle. Cook over medium to medium-high heat. ✧ When the chapati begins to form bubbles (similar to pancakes), turn it over and cook the other side. (If you have a gas stove, continue to cook over a low open flame, rotating and flipping over frequently until large bubbles form.) Continue to turn until done, 2½-3 minutes. ✧ As they are cooked, stack chapatis on top of each other and cover with a cloth, preventing them from drying out and hardening. ✧ Best when served hot.

A thinner, lighter chapati usually served with main dishes in India. If you feel like eating Indian-style, tear off pieces of chapati and use them to pick up tasty morsels of food.

*puja bread*_____

Makes 18

5 c. white flour
1 tsp. baking powder
⅓ c. sugar
½ tsp. salt
1¼ c. water
¼ c. vegetable oil

*Pour flour in a mound on a counter or in a mixing
bowl. Make a hole in the center.* ✧ *Sprinkle baking
powder, sugar, and salt on top.* ✧ *Pour half the
amount of warm water into the hole. With your hand
mix the dry ingredients from the top of the mound
with the water. Work in a circular motion until mixed.
Add the second half of water and repeat the process.
Add the oil and repeat the process until everything is
thoroughly mixed.* ✧ *Knead well for at least 5 minutes. The dough should be well incorporated, not*

sticky. The dough will be heavier and denser than that of the Kopan chapati. Cover and set aside 30 minutes. ✧ On a well-floured surface, knead the dough for a few minutes. With both hands roll the dough into a long sausage shape about 1-½ inches in diameter. Cut into pieces 1 inch wide, or about the width of 2 fingers. ✧ Dust with flour and flatten each piece into a round shape with the palm of your hand. ✧ With a rolling pin, roll out to approximately 6 inches in diameter. ✧ Warm a cast-iron griddle or skillet over medium heat. ✧ Remove excess flour from the chapati by tossing it back and forth in your hands. Place one at a time on the hot griddle. Turn every 30-60 seconds. ✧ Cooking time should be 5-7 minutes. ✧ When cooked, the chapati should feel light. Under-cooked ones will feel heavier.

These chapatis are made especially for pujas — religious ceremonies — at Kopan. They are made as offerings, distributed and eaten during the puja.

puris

❄ *ingredients*

Makes 18

5 c. white flour
1 tsp. baking powder
1 tsp. salt
1 tsp. fresh yeast
1½ c. warm water
oil for deep frying

❄ *method*

*Pour flour in a mound on a counter or in a mixing
bowl. Make a hole in the center.* ○ *Sprinkle baking
powder and salt on top and crumble yeast into the
hole.* ○ *Pour half the amount of warm water into
the hole. With your hand mix the yeast and the water
and gradually work in flour from the top of the mound.
Work in a circular motion until water and dry ingredients are well mixed. Add second half of water and
repeat the process until everything is thoroughly
mixed.* ○ *Knead well for at least 5 minutes. The*

dough should be well incorporated, not sticky. Cover and set aside in a warm place for 1 hour. ○ On a well-floured surface knead the dough for a few minutes. With both hands roll the dough into a long sausage shape about 1½ inches in diameter. Cut into pieces 1 inch wide, or about the width of 2 fingers. ○ Dust with flour and flatten pieces into rounds with the palm of your hand. ○ Roll out as thin as possible to approximately 8 inches in diameter. Remove excess flour by tossing chapati back and forth in your hands, at the same time stretching the dough, making it even thinner. ○ Heat oil in a wok over medium heat. Put a wooden utensil into the oil to test the temperature: when bubbles form, the oil is ready. ○ Holding a chapati with both hands, carefully slide it in from the side of wok, preventing oil from splattering. ○ As soon as the chapati begins to float, spoon hot oil over the top. Turn after 15 seconds and fry for 15 more seconds. ○ Remove and drain on paper towels. Best when served hot.

A deep-fried Kopan chapati.

parathas

✴ *ingredients*

Makes 18

5 c. flour (white or ½ white and ½ wheat)
1 tsp. salt
1½ c. water
oil or butter for pan-frying

stuffed parathas

✴ *ingredients*

Follow recipe for parathas but have on hand 7-8 tablespoons potato momo filling (see page 18).

✴ *method*

Pour flour in a mound on a counter or in a mixing bowl. Make a hole in the center. ☾ *Sprinkle salt on top.* ☾ *Pour half the amount of warm water into the hole. With your hand mix the flour and the water working from the top of the mound. Work in a circular motion until well mixed. Add the second half of water* and repeat the process until flour and water are thoroughly mixed. ◖ Knead for at least 5 minutes. The dough should be well incorporated, not sticky. Cover and set aside 30 minutes. ◖ On a well-floured surface knead the dough a few minutes. With both hands roll the dough into a long sausage shape about 1½ inches in diameter. Cut into pieces 1 inch wide, or about the width of 2 fingers. ◖ Dust with flour and flatten pieces into a round shape with the palm of your hand. ◖ With a rolling pin, roll out to approximately 6 inches in diameter. ◖ Brush oil on half of the dough. ◖ *For Stuffed Parathas, sprinkle 1-2 teaspoons of potato momo filling on the greased half.* ◖ Fold in half and roll. Brush half with oil and fold again. Repeat once. Roll. Parathas should be triangular in shape and thin as a coin. ◖ Heat a cast-iron griddle or skillet over medium heat. Grease with oil or butter. ◖ Place paratha on greased griddle. Brush the top of paratha with oil. ◖ When bubbles form, turn paratha over. Continue to turn until done, 4-6 minutes. ◖ Remove from heat and serve hot.

A delicious pan-fried bread.

kopan tostada _____

❋ *ingredients*

Makes 8

8 Kopan chapatis (see page 74)
1 c. mashed kidney beans or refried beans
½ c. red onion, sliced into rings
1 c. lettuce, shredded
1 c. fresh tomato, diced
1 c. carrot, shredded
2 c. mild white cheese, shredded
Pinch of chili powder
Salt and pepper
Toasted sesame seeds, black or white

Spread beans on top of a chapati. ○ *Layer with the above goodies.* ○ *Sprinkle with chili powder, salt, and pepper.* ○ *To toast sesame seeds, pan-fry without grease over low heat 1-2 minutes.* ○ *Sprinkle sesame seeds over a warm chapati, and serve.*

A chapati topped with fresh vegetables and beans.

cloud momos _____

❋ ingredients

Makes 18

5 c. flour (white or ½ white and ½ wheat)
1 tsp. baking powder
1 tsp. fresh yeast
½ c. warm water
1-2 Tbsp. vegetable oil
1 tsp. salt
⅛ tsp. turmeric

❋ method

*Pour flour in a mound on a counter or in a mixing
bowl. Make a hole in the center. ☾ Sprinkle baking
powder on top and crumble yeast into the hole.
☾ Pour half the amount of warm water into the hole.
With your hand mix the yeast and the water and
gradually work in flour from the top of the mound.
Work in a circular motion until water, yeast, and dry
ingredients are well mixed. Add second half of water*

and repeat the process until everything is thoroughly mixed. ℂ Knead well for at least 5 minutes. The dough should be well incorporated, not sticky. Cover and set aside in a warm place for 1 hour. ℂ Roll out all the dough to a flat rectangle approximately 12 x 18 inches. ℂ Spread oil on top and sprinkle with salt and turmeric, spread ingredients evenly over entire surface. ℂ Roll up, starting with the wider side. ℂ Cut roll into pieces about 2 fingers wide. ℂ Holding a piece of dough with both hands, place your thumbs on each end. Press down with thumbs and stretch dough to 3-4 inches in length. Twist this rectangle once and bring the ends together, forming a twisted fan shape. ℂ Place momos, pinched bottom side down, 1-2 inches apart in a greased steamer. Steam for 15-20 minutes. ℂ Best when served hot.

A "tien" momo (in Tibetan) is a steamed bread twisted into a fan pattern, served as a accompaniment to a main meal.

✻ *condiments*

kopan masala

Makes ½ cup

⅓ c. coriander seeds
¼ c. cumin seeds
10 black cardamom pods, peeled
15 pale green cardamom pods, peeled
25 cloves
2 cinnamon sticks, broken up
1 tsp. black peppercorns
¼ tsp. fresh nutmeg, ground

☼ method

Mix together and grind finely, but not to powder, with a mortar and pestle, rolling pin, coffee grinder or a food processor. ☾ Store in an air-tight jar.

A sweet aromatic mixture of dried spices used in many dishes at Kopan.

kopan peanut butter

ingredients

Makes 1¼ cup

oil for deep-frying
2 c. raw peanuts
¼ c. vegetable oil
½ tsp. salt
2 tsp. sugar

Heat oil in a wok over medium heat. Put a wooden utensil into the oil to test the temperature: when bubbles form, the oil is ready. ✧ *Add peanuts. Cook over a medium-high heat until golden in color. Be careful not to burn or overroast. Allow to cool.* ✧ *Remove from oil. Using a grinder or food processor, coarsely grind the peanuts.* ✧ *Add oil, salt, and sugar. Mix well.* ✧ *Grind the peanut mixture again, until fairly smooth, or as desired.* ✧ *Pour the peanut butter into a container, cover, and store in a cool place.* ✧ *Serve on chapatis with jam. It's great!*

Impossible to find in Asia. A welcome reminder of home.

kopan apple jam _____

❋ *ingredients*

1 part apples, peeled and chopped
water
1 part sugar
lemons, if desired

Place apples in a saucepan. Add enough water to almost cover the fruit. If desired, add a few finely chopped lemons — this makes the jam set better. ◯ *Bring to boil and simmer until fruit is soft.* ◯ *Add as much sugar by weight as you have apples. Boil very quickly, until jam sets or becomes thick enough to use.* ◯ *Pour jam into sterilized jars.*

Note: Kancha often adds other fruits, such as bananas, papayas, or whatever's available.

A great topping for chapatis.

kancha's salad dressing

❋ *ingredients*

Makes ⅓ cup

2 Tbsp. lemon juice
2 Tbsp. vegetable oil
2 Tbsp. water
1 tsp. fresh garlic, minced
2 tsp. salt
1 tsp. sugar
¼ tsp. ground black pepper
¼ tsp. chili powder

Mix all ingredients in a small jar and shake well. Pour over salad, toss, and serve.

Kancha serves this dressing on sliced cucumber, sliced carrots, and red onion rings.

spicy salad dressing———————

Makes ½ cup

4 cloves, whole
4 pale green cardamom pods, peeled
¼ c. vegetable oil
2 Tbsp. white vinegar
⅛ c. soy sauce
½ Tbsp. fresh ginger root, minced
½ Tbsp. fresh garlic, minced
1 tsp. sugar
¼ tsp. salt
1 tsp. Kopan masala (see page 92)
⅛ tsp. chili powder
⅛ tsp. ground black pepper

With rolling pin or mortar and pestle, or food pro-cessor, crush cloves and cardamom. ☾ Combine all ingredients in a small saucepan. ☾ Bring to boil over medium heat. Allow to simmer on low heat for 1 minute. ☾ Remove from heat and allow to cool. ☾ Mix well just before pouring over salad. ☾ Toss well and serve.

✹ *teas*

kopan milk tea

Makes 4 cups

3 c. water
1 c. milk
5 slices fresh ginger root (coin size)
4 cinnamon sticks
6 pale green cardamom pods, peeled
1 Tbsp. tea leaves, Darjeeling or a similar black tea
3 Tbsp. sugar

✤ *method*

In a saucepan, bring water, ginger, cinnamon, and cardamom seeds to a boil. ☾ *Add tea leaves and remove from heat. Allow to steep 5 minutes.* ☾ *Add hot milk.* ☾ *Add sugar to taste.* ☾ *Pour through a strainer. Serve hot.*

A wonderfully spiced tea. The most popular hot drink at Kopan.

tibetan butter tea _____

✸ *ingredients*

Makes 4 cups

3 c. water
1 Tbsp. tea leaves, Darjeeling or a similar black tea
¼ c. butter
1 c. milk
1½ tsp. salt

In a saucepan bring water to a boil. ✧ *Add tea leaves and remove from heat. Allow to steep 5 minutes.* ✧ *In another saucepan, melt butter in hot milk and mix well. Add to tea.* ✧ *Add salt to taste.* ✧ *Strain into a blender. Blend until frothy. Serve hot.*

The national hot drink of Tibet and a favorite among the monks and nuns. Initially, a shock to the Western taste buds expecting "tea;" in time, you develop a taste for it. Tibetans usually use a Chinese brick tea; otherwise, use Darjeeling or a similar black tea.

mint tea

❋ ingredients

Makes 4 cups

4 c. water
2 c. fresh mint leaves
2-2½ Tbsp. sugar

☀ *m e t h o d*

In a saucepan, bring water to a boil. ☾ Add mint leaves and simmer 10 minutes. ☾ Allow to steep 5 minutes. ☾ Add sugar to taste. ☾ Pour through a strainer. Serve hot or cold.

The longer it steeps, the better.

For lemon tea use 1 Tbsp. tea leaves, Darjeeling or a similar black tea, and add lemon juice and sugar to taste.

glossary of spices _____

Bay leaves: Dried leaves of the laurel tree. Sweet-smelling when cooked. Used frequently in Mediterranean and Indian cooking. Can be purchased in Italian, Greek, or Indian grocery stores.

Cardamom: There are two kinds: a large black variety and a small pale green one. Used to give a sweet flavor to dishes. Pods can be purchased in Indian grocery stores.

Chili powder: Dried, roasted, and ground chilies. They vary in hotness from country to country, so use sparingly at first.

Cinnamon: The bark of a tropical Asian tree. Used for giving a sweet taste and aroma to food. Readily available in sticks or powder.

Cloves: The dried unopened flower of a tropical Asian plant. Used whole or powdered to give food a pungent flavor and aroma. Readily available.

Coriander: A member of the parsley family. Ground coriander seeds are one of the main ingredients in curry powders, and the fresh leaves are used for flavoring and garnishing dishes. Also known as Chinese parsley or cilantro. Commonly used throughout Asia, Mexico, and the Mediterranean. Easily grown in your herb garden; seeds are available at Asian grocery stores.

Cumin: Whole or ground, has a robust flavor and is used in spicy dishes throughout the world. A popular ingredient in curry powders and masalas. Readily available.

Curry Powder: A Western term used to refer to a prepackaged standard blend of crushed dried spices and herbs. Varies in degree of hotness.

Garlic: Essential in Asian cooking. Use fresh. Remove skin by smashing the clove with the side of cleaver, then chop or mince. To store peeled whole cloves, chopped or minced garlic, place in a small jar and cover with oil. Use the oil for stir-frying and in salad dressings.

Ginger: A root that gives a hot, spicy flavor. Also essential in Asian cooking. Use peeled. To mince, smash with the side of a cleaver, then chop very finely. To store, keep in a jar, covered with sherry, or freeze. If not found at your local grocery store, try Asian or Indian grocers.

Indian Tomato Red Powder: Powdered red food coloring in a tin, made in India by Bush Boake Allen (India) Ltd. Try Indian grocers; if not available then liquid red food coloring can be used as a substitute.

Masala: A mixture of dried aromatic spices used throughout India and Nepal. Each family, village, and region has its own blends. Available packaged at Indian grocers, but the fragrance and taste of homemade masala are well worth the time and trouble.

Nutmeg: A small, hard, sweet-smelling seed from an Indian ever-green. Use sparingly. Available whole or ground. Whole nuts must be finely grated before use. Readily available.

Turmeric: A member of the ginger family, also known as Indian saffron. A yellow powder, one of the main ingredients in curries. Can be found in Indian grocery stores.

index

A complete list of all ingredients mentioned in book:

apples
baking powder
bay leaves
black cardamom pods
black pepercorns
broccoli
butter
cabbage
carrot
cashew nuts
chili powder
Chinese parsley/cilantro
cinnamon sticks
cloves
coconut flakes

coriander seeds
corn starch
cream corn (canned)
cumin seeds
Darjeeling (or other black) tea
dry egg noodles
dry lentils
eggs
flour, wheat
flour, white
fresh bean sprouts
fresh spinach
fresh tomatos
frying oil
garlic
ginger root
green beans
green cardamom pods
green onions (scallions)
ground black pepper
ground cinnamon
ground nutmeg
hot curry powder
Indian Tomato Red Powder
ketchup (optional)
lemon juice
lemons (optional)
lettuce
mild white cheese (Jack or Mozzerella)
milk
mint leaves
mixed vegetables (most often
    cauliflower, spinach, cabbage, etc.)
mushrooms
peas
potatos

pumpkin
raisins
raw peanuts
red kidney beans (fresh or canned)
red onions
salt
sesame seeds, black & white
soy sauce
squash
string beans
sugar
Swiss cheese
tofu
turmeric
vegetable oil
white rice, long grained
white vinegar
yeast

*Complete list of all utensils
mentioned:*

blendor
bowls
cast iron skillet, 12-inch & small
deep fry pan
knives
noodle machine
nortar & pestle or grinder
rolling pin
sauce pans, large & small
steamer
wire whisk
wok
wooden utensil